# GAME ON!

# CHESS
# FOR BEGINNERS

## JON TREMAINE

WINDMILL
BOOKS ™

# INTRODUCTION

Chess is the world's most popular board game. It is played in every country in the world and is thought to have originated in India about 1,400 years ago.

Simply stated, the object of the game is to capture your opponent's king before he captures yours. What is the fascination of chess? Well, it is a very easy game to learn to play, but an extremely difficult game to learn to play well. The best players in the world still have to practice every day. However, it's a really enjoyable game at any level!

In introducing you to this wonderful game, the explanations have been kept as simple as possible, so you can begin playing right away.

Just learn the rules of the game and how the pieces move. Don't panic — it's easier than you think!

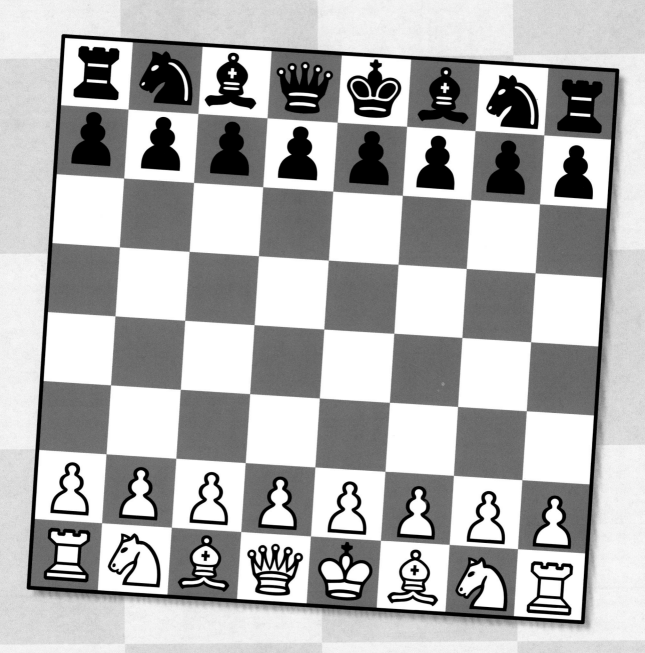

Go find yourself an opponent!

## GOOD LUCK!

# THE BOARD

Chess is a game for two players, known as white and black. The game is played on a chessboard containing 64 squares laid out in eight rows of eight squares. They alternate between light-colored and dark-colored squares. Horizontal lines of squares are called ranks, vertical lines are called files, and diagonal lines, which can vary from two to eight squares, are called diagonals.

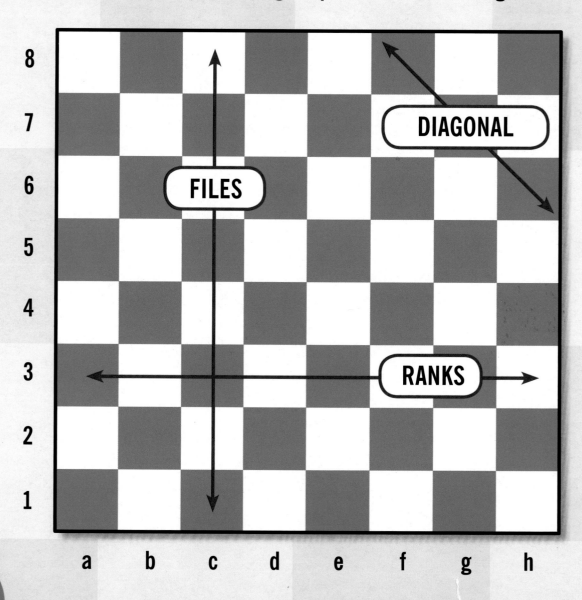

# THE PIECES

Both players have an army of sixteen pieces: a king, a queen, two bishops, two knights, two rooks, and eight pawns.

**KING**

**QUEEN**

**ROOK**

**BISHOP**

**KNIGHT**

**PAWN**

**KING**

**QUEEN**

**ROOK**

**BISHOP**

**KNIGHT**

**PAWN**

5

# THE SETUP

You must arrange the board so that you have a white square in the bottom right-hand corner. This is how the pieces are laid out:

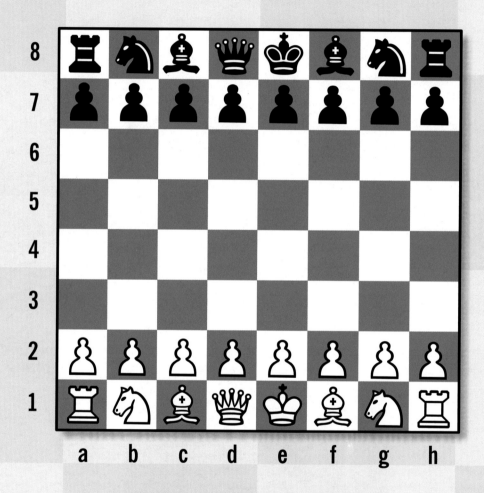

## OBJECT OF THE GAME

The object of the game is to "capture" your opponent's king by forcing him into a position where he is directly threatened, only able to move into a square that is also directly threatened, and cannot be defended by another member of his army. When this happens, the game is lost. This is called "checkmate."

# NOTATION

Notation is the way to identify each of the 64 squares on the board. It also allows us to identify the moves made in the game. The ranks (horizontals) are numbered from 1 to 8. The files (verticals) are lettered a to h. The fifth square along the "a" file is called a5. The third square along the "d" file is called d3. Simple, isn't it?

White's move and black's reply can be represented as follows:

1. e4   c6
2. d4   d5

Remember, white always moves first. Your board should now look like this:

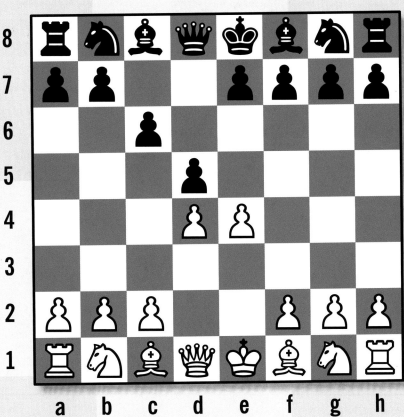

The chess pieces are identified by their initial letters:

# K = King, Q = Queen, B = Bishop,
# R = Rook, and Kt or N = Knight.

The poor old pawn isn't given an initial!
You merely indicate the identity of the square that it moves to.

• • • • • • • • • • • • • • • • • • • • • • • • • • • • • • • •

Set up your board and follow the opening game below.

Move the pieces for
both white and black…

1. d4 d5
2. c4 e6
3. Nc3 Nf6
4. Bg5 Be7

Your board should
now look like this:

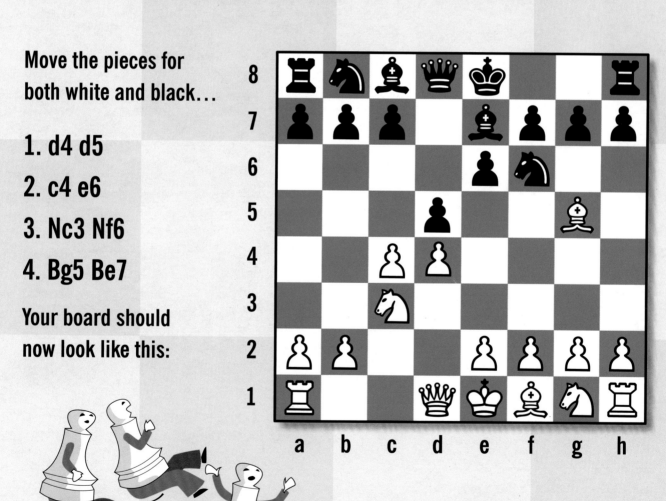

# THE STRENGTH OF THE PIECES

You must learn to figure out who has the strongest position and game at any point of play. The queen is the most powerful and dangerous piece because she can reach every corner of the board very quickly. Remember the comparative value and strength of each piece.

 **A pawn is worth 1 point.**

 **A knight is worth 3 points.**

 **A bishop is worth 3 points.**

 **A rook is worth 5 points.**

 **A queen is worth 9 points.**

The king has a special role and can only be graded on his aggressive value, which is about equal to a knight or a bishop.

Don't underestimate the poor old pawn, because its value increases the closer it gets to the eighth rank. Promotion can instantly change it into a queen, which is worth nine points.

# THE KING'S MOVE

Just to be difficult, the six different pieces move in different ways! Let's look at the king. He can only move one square at a time – but this can be in any direction: forward, backward, to either side, or diagonally.

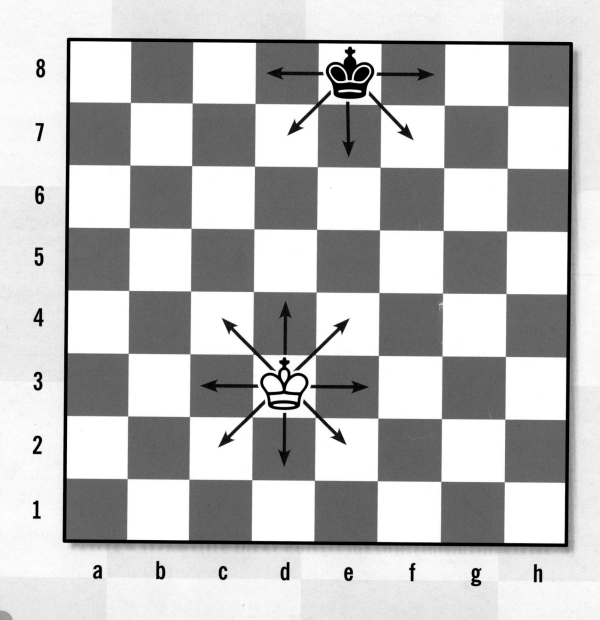

Since the king can only move one square at a time, it can only capture a piece that lies on an adjacent square. The piece is removed from the board, and the king occupies the now-vacant square.

# THE QUEEN'S MOVE

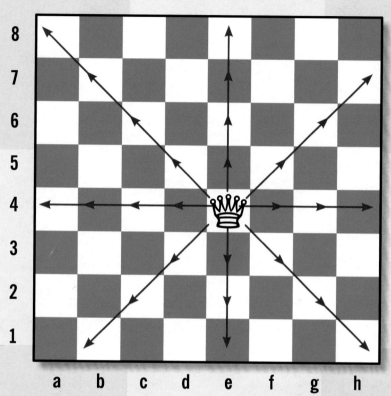

The queen is the most powerful chess piece. She can move anywhere in a straight line – horizontally, vertically, or diagonally.

She threatens any opposing piece that sits on any of the squares that are directly in her way.

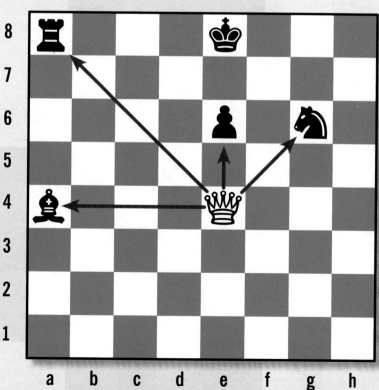

# THE BISHOP'S MOVE

The bishop can only move and capture diagonally. You have two bishops, and they are very powerful pieces in chess.

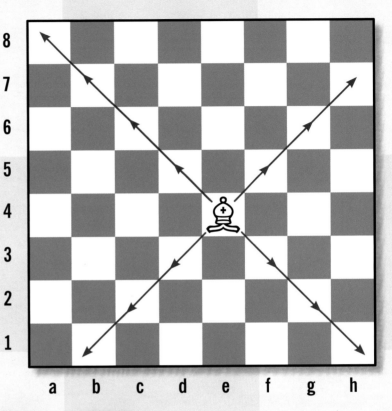

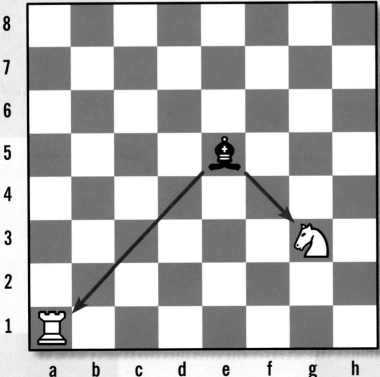

Here, the black bishop is attacking the white rook and knight at the same time. White can only move one of them — so the other one will be lost to the crafty bishop.

# THE KNIGHT'S MOVE

The knight is represented by a horse. The knight is the only chess piece that can jump over other pieces. It has an unusual move: two steps along a horizontal rank or a vertical file and then one step to either side. A knight always lands on a different-colored square than the one he came from.

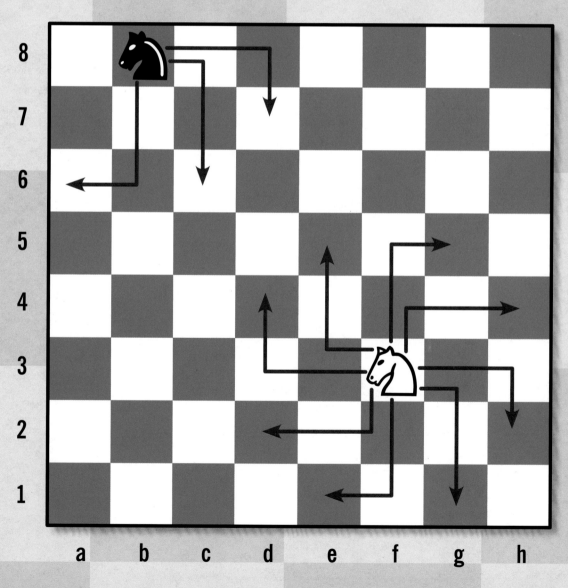

Although the knight can
jump over other pieces,
it can only capture a piece
that is sitting on the last
square that it lands on.

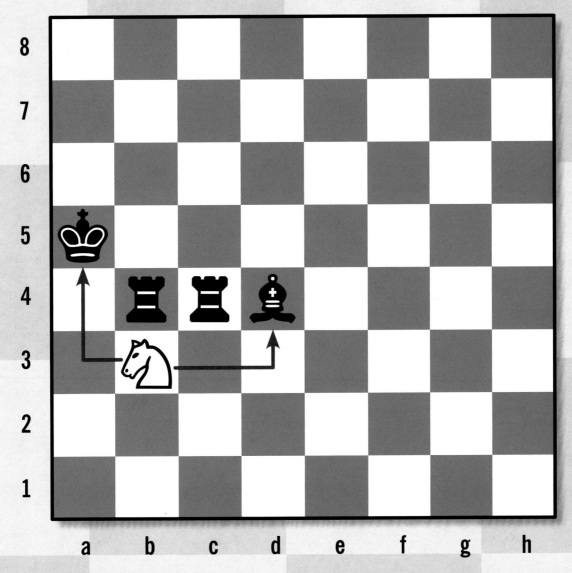

# THE ROOK'S MOVE

Rooks used to be called castles. The name was changed because of the confusion with the expression and action of "castling," which will be explained later. The rook's power should never be underestimated and, when properly utilized, can launch a formidable attack. Rooks only move along the horizontal ranks and vertical files. They can move any number of vacant squares.

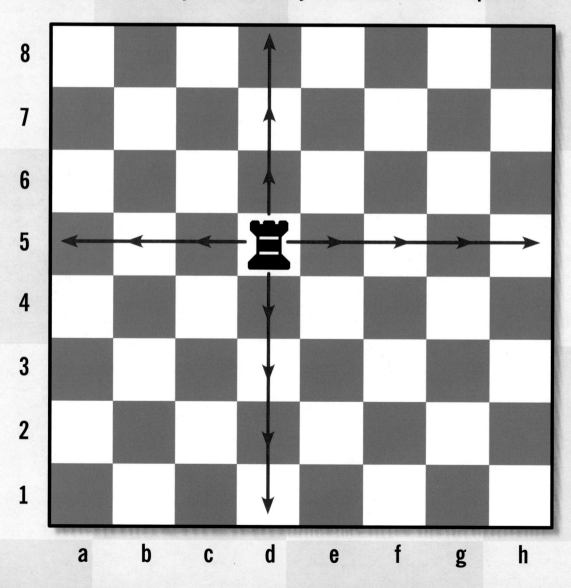

A rook may capture any opponent's piece that is directly in its path. The piece is removed from the board, and the rook takes its place.

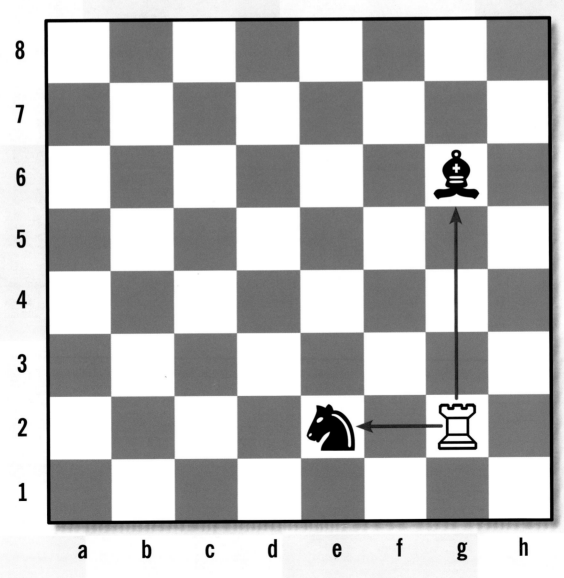

# THE PAWN'S MOVE

Each side has eight pawns, which are positioned in a line across the second horizontal rank. You have the option of moving a pawn either one or two squares forward along the vertical file on its first move only. After each pawn's first move, it may only move forward one square at a time.

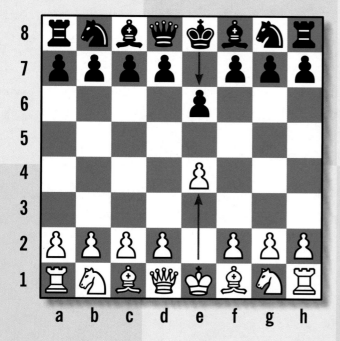

**Pawns can only capture diagonally:**

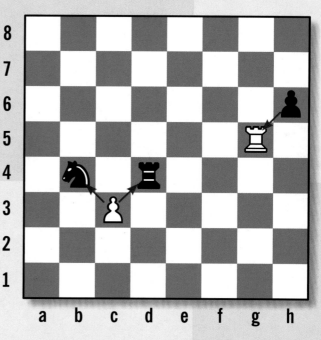

# EN PASSANT

En passant means "in passing" and is the second way for a pawn to capture another pawn. If, on its opening move, a pawn moves two places in order to avoid being captured, and in doing this passes over the attacked diagonal square of an opponent's pawn, it can be captured as if it had only moved one place.

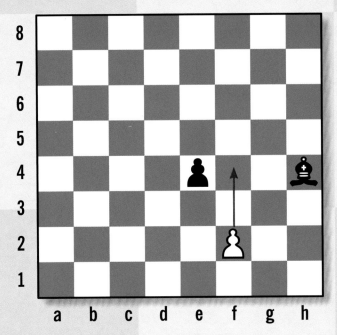

The attacking piece moves into the square that it would have occupied if the attacked pawn had only moved one place and had been captured in the normal way. En passant must be made immediately after the offending pawn has made its double forward move. If you move another one of your pieces after this move, you forfeit the right of en passant.

# OPENING MOVES

White always plays first. His eight pawns can be moved forward one or two squares, and his two knights each have a choice of two squares to aim for.

It is common to start with a pawn move to exert pressure and control upon the center of the board. Pieces placed in the central area of the board control a much wider area than those at the side of the board.

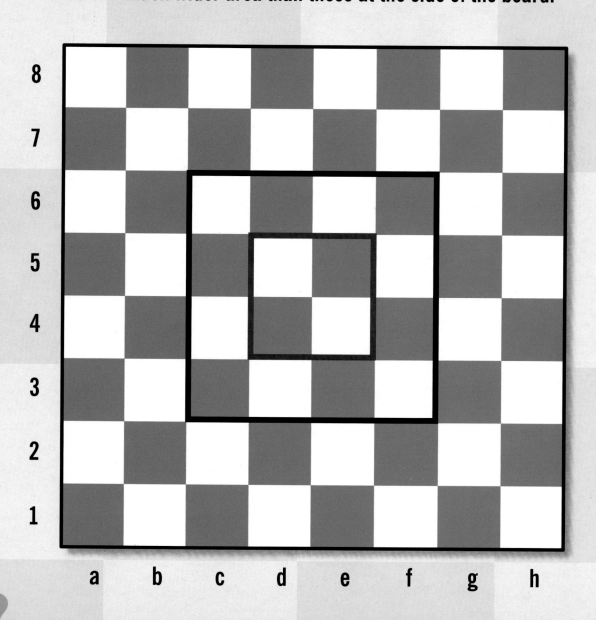

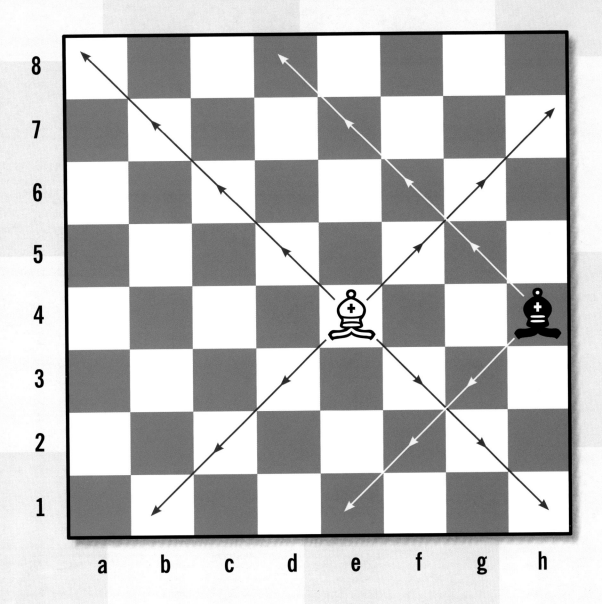

Notice how much more territory the white bishop controls than the black bishop: fourteen squares for white and only eight for black.

# ♛ QUEENING

When a pawn reaches the eighth rank, it cannot go forward any further, so a new and exciting rule comes into play. The rules of the game specify that it can no longer remain a pawn but instead can become any piece on the board, with the exception of a king. This change is called a "promotion." The lowly pawn can now become a powerful queen.

Often a player will have two queens in play, and with them, can launch a devastating combined attack. Three or four queens are possible; nine queens, although possible, are unheard of. Use a token or an inverted rook to represent your extra queen.

**REMEMBER:**
Promoting a pawn to another piece other than a queen should always be carefully considered. A queen is not always the best option.

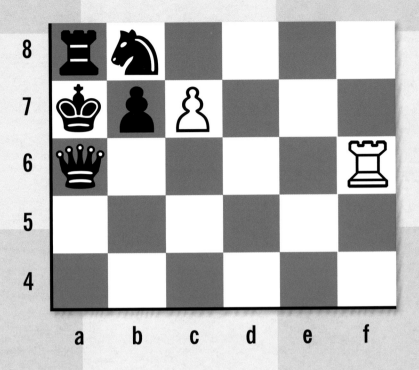

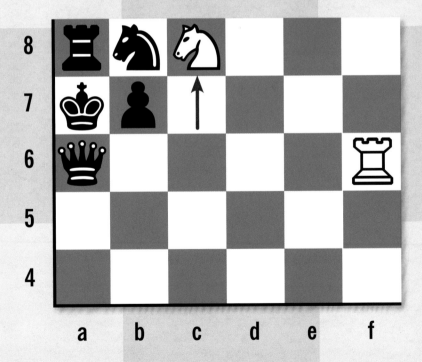

Here, promoting the pawn to a knight instantly wins the game for white.

# ♖ CASTLING

Your rooks are positioned at the far ends of your home rank. They are much more useful if they are operating near the center of the board. A special move has been created to make this possible. This move is called castling.

Castling brings the rook into the center of the board, and at the same time, moves your king into a safer area.

Providing that there are no other pieces between the rook and the king, the king moves two squares toward the rook. The rook is now lifted and placed on the other side of the king.

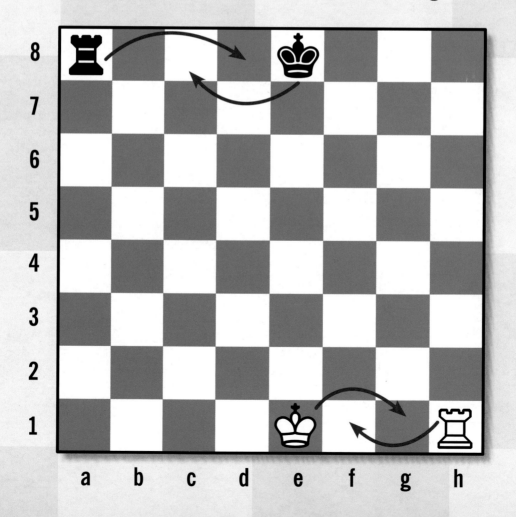

**Here, white has castled on his king's side and black has castled on his queen's side.**

**Five situations can arise that would make castling illegal:**

### 1. If the king has already moved.

### 2. If the rook has already moved.

### 3. If the square on which the king stands is under attack.

### 4. If the square that the king must cross is under attack.

### 5. If the square that the king would land on is under attack.

# CHECK

If your king is captured, you immediately lose the game. Therefore, he must be protected at all costs. When the king's square is directly threatened by an opposing piece, it is said to be "in check." In order to prevent the king from being captured, several options are available to you:

 Move to a square that is not threatened.

 Move another piece into the firing line.

 Immediately capture the threatening piece.

Here, the white king is threatened by the black rook:

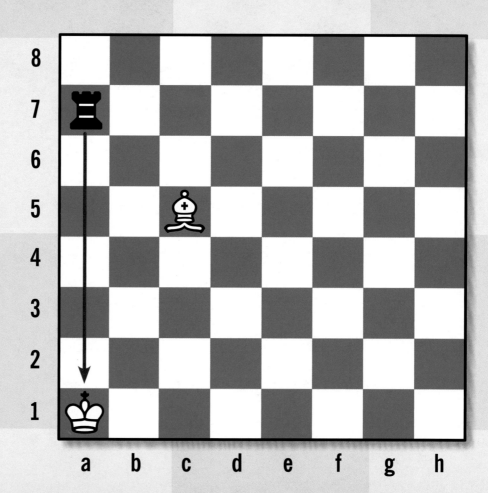

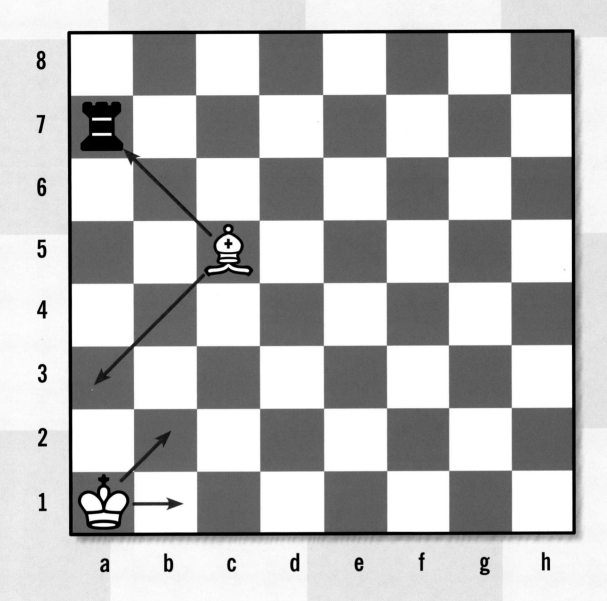

White's three options are:

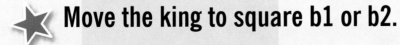 Move the king to square b1 or b2.

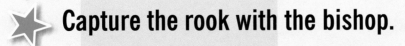 Capture the rook with the bishop.

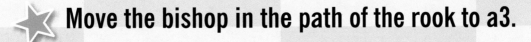 Move the bishop in the path of the rook to a3.

# CHECKMATE

Checkmate is the goal that you must always strive to achieve. When a king is in check (directly threatened) and there is no move that can be made to get him out of check, the game is over. The player whose king is in check loses. This position is called checkmate. In the example, the white rook at d8 checks the black king. The king cannot escape to another square. All his escape routes are covered. He cannot capture the rook with his knight because it would leave the king open to attack from white's bishop at a2. He cannot move his knight to f8 for the same reason. Victory for white!

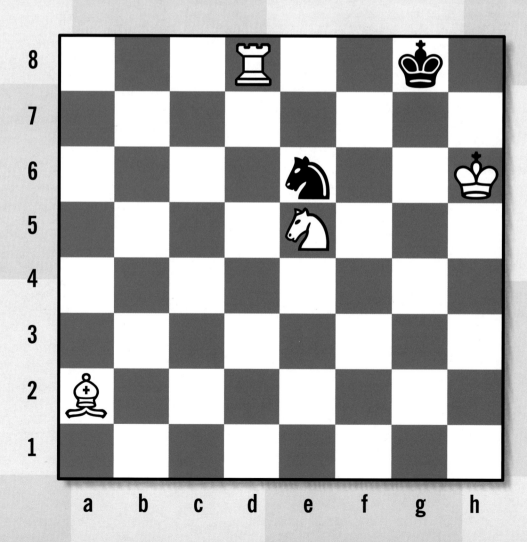

**Here are three more examples of checkmate on the black king:**

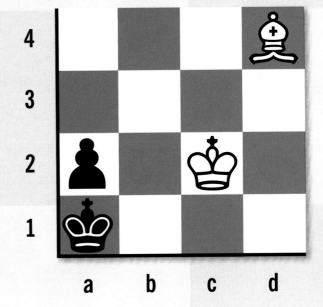

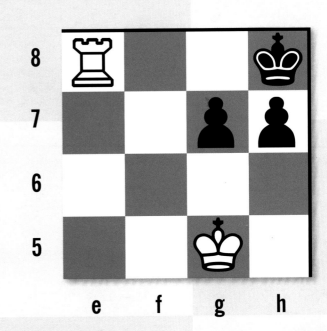

# DRAWN GAMES

If your king is not in check and you have no legal moves left, the game is drawn. This is called "stalemate." A losing game can often be turned into a drawn game by hunting out a stalemate situation. Here are a few examples. In each case it is black's move:

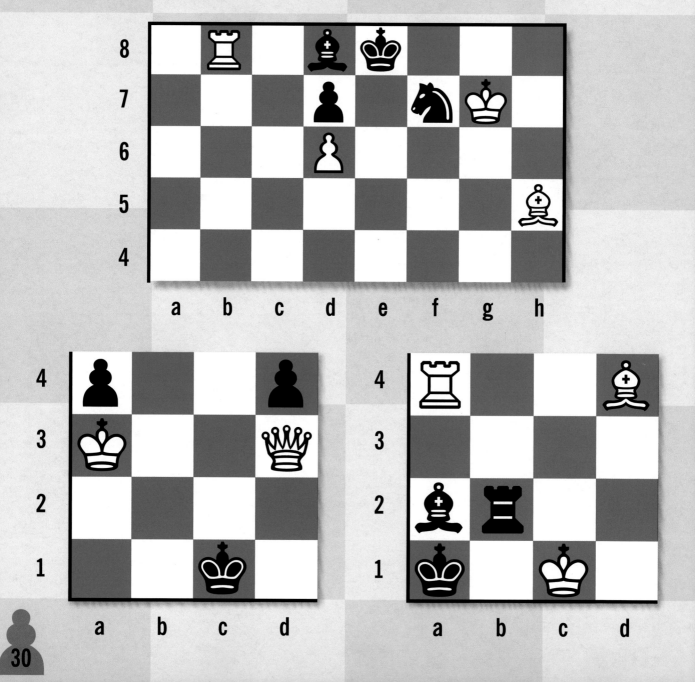

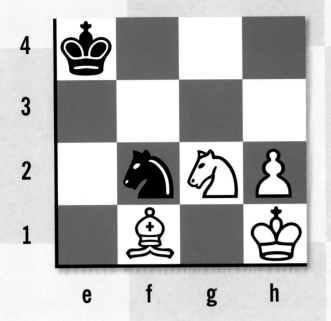

Perpetual check also results in a drawn game. Here, the white king is being attacked by black's knight on f2. He can only move the knight to g1. Black now moves his knight to h3 and the king is in check again. This could go on forever, so a draw is called.

A draw can also be agreed between the players if:

 neither has a realistic chance of winning.

 three identical moves have been made in succession, with no progress.

 50 moves have been made by each side with no captures.

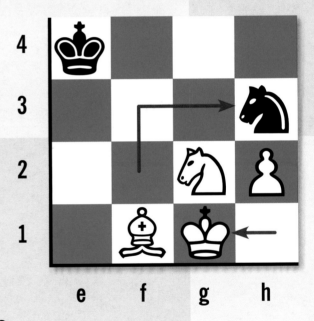

# WHAT NEXT?

The purpose of this book is to whet your appetite for the wonderful game of chess and, more importantly, to get you playing. There is no room in a book of this length to teach you strategy; to teach you more good opening moves; to tell you about scholar's mate and fool's mate; or to explain the technique of discovered check and forked attacks, pins and skewers, and so on.

Once you become familiar with the rules and moves, and have played a few games, go to your bookstore or library and read as much as you can. There is so much more to learn about this fantastic game, and you will never regret the time you put into mastering it.

You will never know it all. Even the chess grand masters are still learning and have to practice every day!

Published in 2022 by Windmill Books,
an Imprint of Rosen Publishing
29 East 21st Street, New York, NY 10010

Copyright © 2022 iSeek Ltd.

Cataloging-in-Publication Data

Names: Tremaine, Jon.
Title: Chess for beginners / Jon Tremaine.
Description: New York : Windmill Books, 2022. | Series: Game on!
Identifiers: ISBN 9781538270097 (pbk.) | ISBN 9781538270110 (library bound) | ISBN 9781538270103 (6 pack) | ISBN 9781538270127 (ebook)
Subjects: LCSH: Chess–Juvenile literature.
Classification: LCC GV1446.T75 2022 | DDC 794.1–dc23

Manufactured in the United States of America

CPSIA Compliance Information: Batch BSWM22: For Further Information contact Rosen Publishing, New York, New York at 1-800-237-9932